D1810253

Myraki Publishing

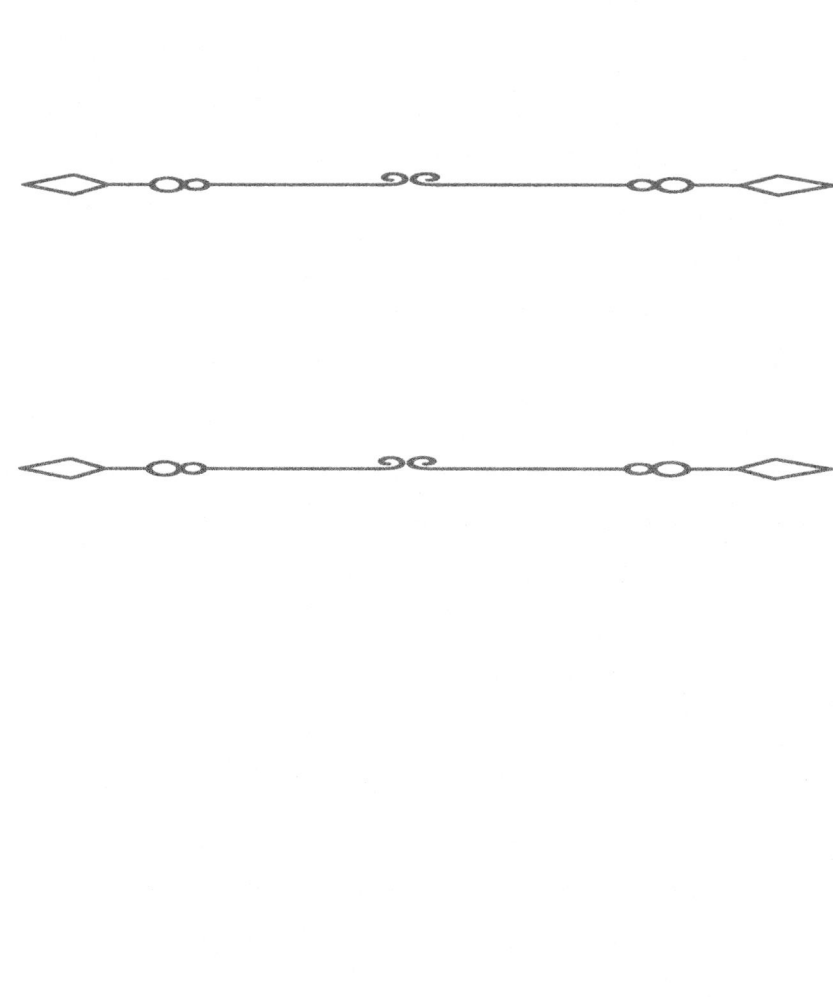

Vow not to keep score, even when you
are totally winning.

The madness of love is the greatest of
heaven's blessings.

- Plato

When you're wrong, admit it. When
you're right, be quiet.

Marriage is not finding a perfect person;
it's finding a person perfect for you.

Marriage is successful when the hap-
piness of your partner is
essential to your own.

If you feel the urge to yell at your spouse,
try having something to eat.

True love may start a beautiful marriage, but true friendship sustains it.

———

———

———

———

———

———

———

———

———

———

———

———

———

———

———

———

———

———

———

———

———

◇──∞────────᧤᧧────────∞──◇

A smart woman will never start a
fight with a man who is cleaning.

◇──∞────────᧤᧧────────∞──◇

Never, ever yell at each other
...unless the house is on fire.

Never stop dating each other.

You don't have to think alike to
have a successful marriage, but
you have to think together.

What counts in making a happy marriage
is not so much how compatible you are, but
how you deal with incompatibility.

- Leo Tolstoy

There is no remedy for love but
to love more.

- Henry David Thoreau

Love is not blind, it sees but
it doesn't mind.

If you tell the truth you never have
to remember anything.

- Mark Twain

Printed in Great Britain
by Amazon

11625465R00058